BLACK GOLD STRANGLEHOLD